OCEAN LIFE UP CLOSE

Great White Sharks

by Rebecca Pettiford

BLASTOFF!
3
READERS

BELLWETHER MEDIA · MINNEAPOLIS, MN

Note to Librarians, Teachers, and Parents:

Blastoff! Readers are carefully developed by literacy experts and combine standards-based content with developmentally appropriate text.

Level 1 provides the most support through repetition of high-frequency words, light text, predictable sentence patterns, and strong visual support.

Level 2 offers early readers a bit more challenge through varied simple sentences, increased text load, and less repetition of high-frequency words.

Level 3 advances early-fluent readers toward fluency through increased text and concept load, less reliance on visuals, longer sentences, and more literary language.

Level 4 builds reading stamina by providing more text per page, increased use of punctuation, greater variation in sentence patterns, and increasingly challenging vocabulary.

Level 5 encourages children to move from "learning to read" to "reading to learn" by providing even more text, varied writing styles, and less familiar topics.

Whichever book is right for your reader, Blastoff! Readers are the perfect books to build confidence and encourage a love of reading that will last a lifetime!

This edition first published in 2017 by Bellwether Media, Inc.

No part of this publication may be reproduced in whole or in part without written permission of the publisher. For information regarding permission, write to Bellwether Media, Inc., Attention: Permissions Department, 5357 Penn Avenue South, Minneapolis, MN 55419.

Library of Congress Cataloging-in-Publication Data

Names: Pettiford, Rebecca, author.
Title: Great White Sharks / by Rebecca Pettiford.
Description: Minneapolis, MN : Bellwether Media, Inc., [2017] | Series:
   Blastoff! Readers. Ocean Life Up Close | Audience: Ages 5-8. | Audience: K to
   grade 3. | Includes bibliographical references and index.
Identifiers: LCCN 2015045876 | ISBN 9781626174160 (hardcover : alk. paper)
Subjects: LCSH: White shark–Juvenile literature.
Classification: LCC QL638.95.L3 P48 2017 | DDC 597.3/3–dc23
LC record available at http://lccn.loc.gov/2015045876

Printed in the United States of America, North Mankato, MN.

Table of
Contents

What Are Great White Sharks?

Great white sharks are the biggest **predatory** fish on Earth. They look like **torpedoes** and can weigh 5,000 pounds (2,268 kilograms)!

Other Mackerel Sharks

thresher sharks

sand sharks

basking sharks

These **carnivores** are in a group called **mackerel sharks**.

Great whites live in warm and cool waters. Most stay close to shore to feed on **prey**.

Sometimes, they **migrate** thousands of miles to find food.

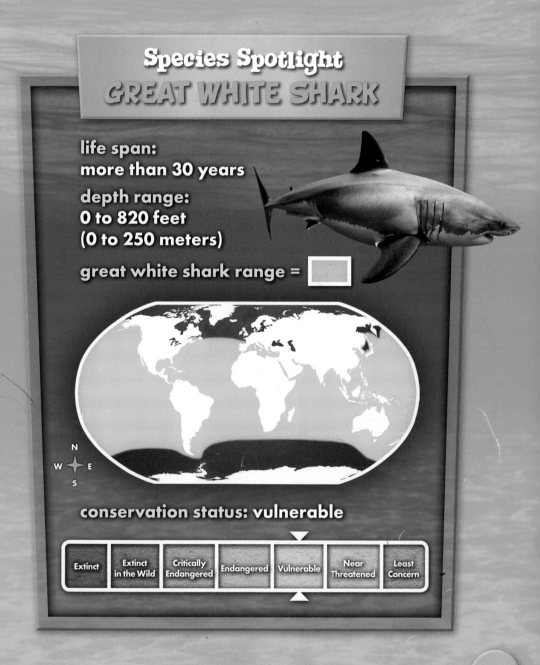

Species Spotlight
GREAT WHITE SHARK

life span:
more than 30 years

depth range:
**0 to 820 feet
(0 to 250 meters)**

great white shark range =

N
W · E
S

conservation status: **vulnerable**

Extinct	Extinct in the Wild	Critically Endangered	Endangered	Vulnerable	Near Threatened	Least Concern

Deadly and Fast

The teeth of great whites are **serrated** and triangular. Narrow bottom teeth hold prey. Large upper teeth cut chunks of meat.

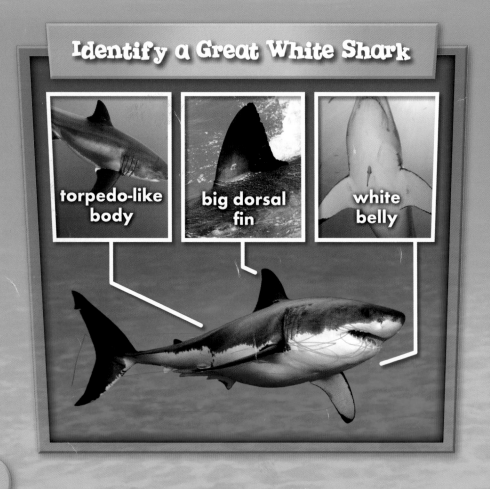

Identify a Great White Shark

torpedo-like body

big dorsal fin

white belly

These predators can replace lost teeth with new ones.

gills

These sharks can be 20 feet (6.1 meters) long! Their bodies are made of bendable **cartilage**. This helps them speed through the water.

Great white sharks are always on the move. They need to swim so their **gills** can take in air.

Great White Shark Size

average
human

15 to 20 feet
(4.6 to 6.1 meters) long

Great whites use many fins to move. The big **dorsal fin** keeps them from rolling over.

dorsal fin

tail fin

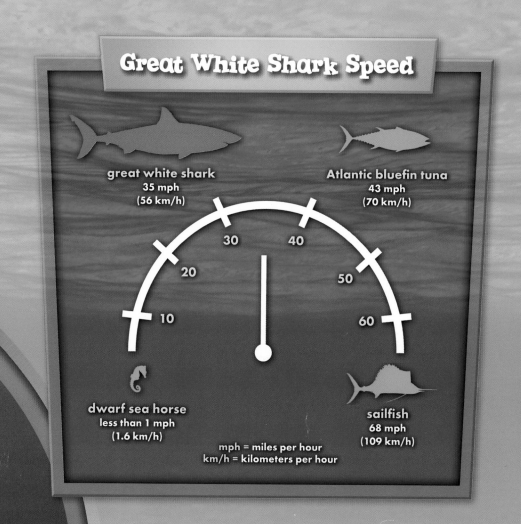

Great White Shark Speed

great white shark
35 mph
(56 km/h)

Atlantic bluefin tuna
43 mph
(70 km/h)

30   40

20   50

10   60

dwarf sea horse
less than 1 mph
(1.6 km/h)

sailfish
68 mph
(109 km/h)

mph = miles per hour
km/h = kilometers per hour

The tail fin pushes them forward. Great whites swim in bursts up to 35 miles (56 kilometers) per hour to catch prey!

Coloring on these sharks helps them hunt. White bellies make them hard to see against the sunlit surface.

Their dark backs blend in with the ocean's bottom.

Inside the shark's body, two **lateral lines** run from the head to the tail fin.

The lines help great whites sense the movements of other animals.

Great whites can smell blood from miles away. They feast on stingrays, sea turtles, and small whales.

The sharks also like to hunt seals and sea lions. They shoot out of the water with jaws open wide!

Catch of the Day

beluga
whales

green
sea turtles

Steller
sea lions

Shark Pups

Female sharks carry eggs inside their bodies for about a year. Then they birth two to ten baby sharks.

The newborn **pups** are up to 5 feet (1.5 meters) long. They are ready to hunt!

Glossary

carnivores—animals that only eat meat

cartilage—a strong, bendable material that makes up most of a shark's body

dorsal fin—a fin on top of a shark's back; great white sharks have two dorsal fins.

gills—the breathing parts of sharks that get air from water

lateral lines—lines along each side of a great white shark that can feel the movements of other animals

mackerel sharks—sharks that have two dorsal fins, five gill openings, and a mouth that usually reaches past their eyes; great whites, makos, and threshers are all mackerel sharks.

migrate—to travel from one place to another, often with the seasons

predatory—living by hunting other animals for food

prey—animals that are hunted by other animals for food

pups—baby great white sharks

serrated—having a sawlike edge

torpedoes—tube-shaped weapons fired underwater

To Learn More

AT THE LIBRARY

Barnes, Nico. *Great White Sharks*. Minneapolis, Minn.: Abdo Kids, 2015.

Green, Jen. *Great White Shark*. New York, N.Y.: Bearport Pub., 2014.

Loh-Hagan, Virginia. *Discover Great White Sharks*. Ann Arbor, Mich.: Cherry Lake Publishing, 2016.

ON THE WEB

Learning more about great white sharks is as easy as 1, 2, 3.

1. Go to www.factsurfer.com.

2. Enter "great white sharks" into the search box.

3. Click the "Surf" button and you will see a list of related web sites.

With factsurfer.com, finding more information is just a click away.

Index